Table of Contents

Peek Inside a Pencil   3

Photo Glossary   15

Index   16

About the Author   16

Can you find these words?

barrel

cedar

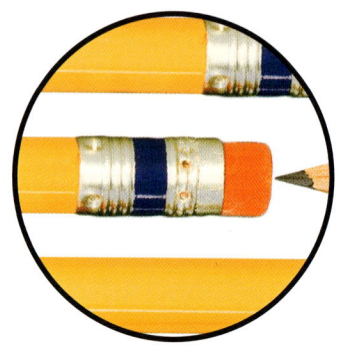

eraser

graphite

Peek Inside a Pencil

Peek inside a pencil.
What do you see?

I see the **barrel**.

cedar

It is made of **cedar**.

graphite

Peek inside a pencil. What do you see?

I see **graphite**.
This is the pencil's lead.

Peek inside a pencil.
What can't you see?

Glue holds the parts together.

Peek outside a pencil.
What do you see?

I see paint. I see an **eraser**.

eraser

Peek outside a pencil.
What do you see?

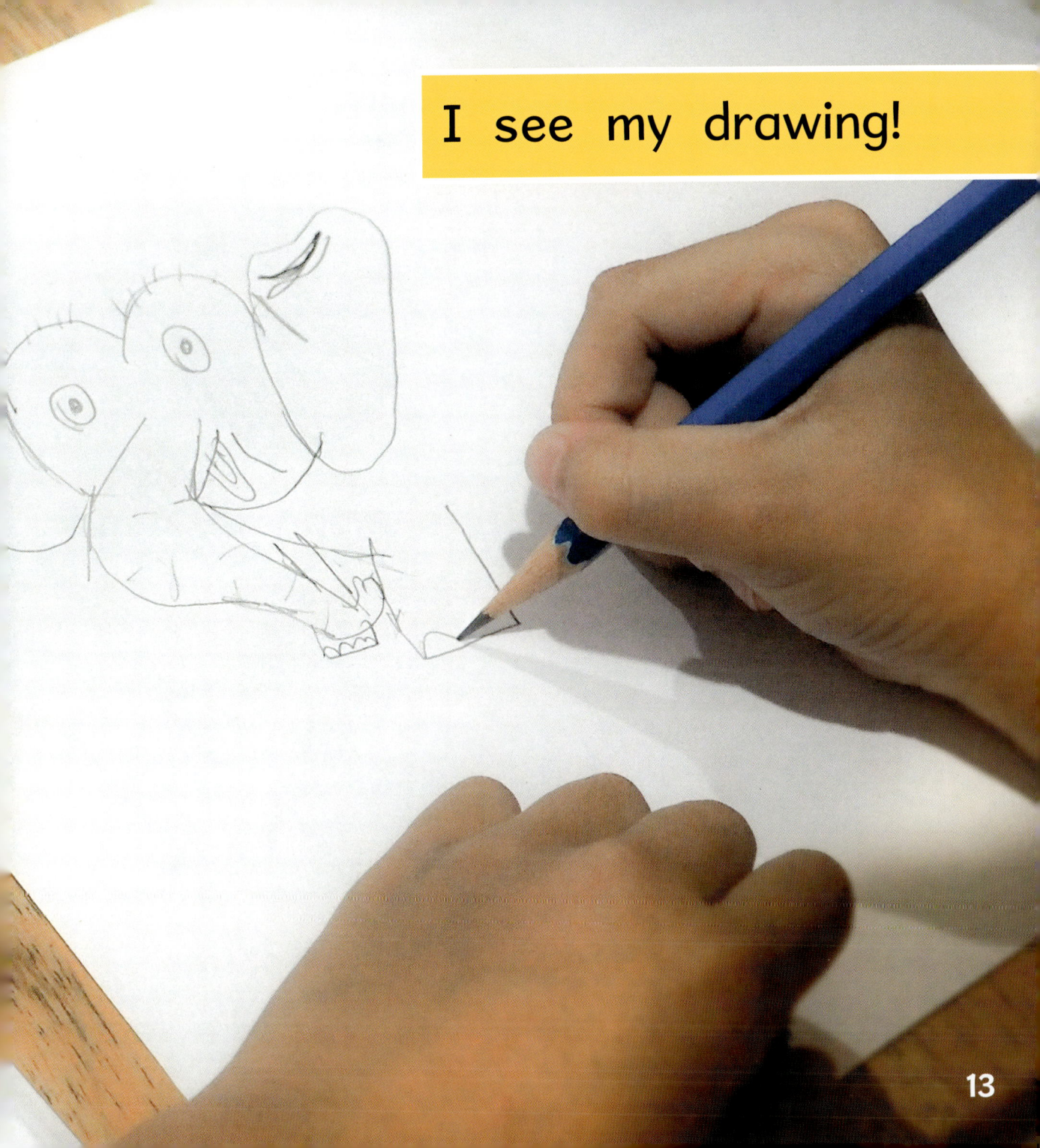
I see my drawing!

Did you find these words?

I see the **barrel**.

It is made of **cedar**.

I see paint. I see an **eraser**.

I see **graphite**. This is the pencil's lead.

Photo Glossary

 **barrel** (BAR-uhl): A tube-shaped part of something.

 **cedar** (SEE-dur): A type of evergreen tree with needles as leaves.

 **eraser** (i-RAY-sur): Something used to remove pencil or chalk marks.

 **graphite** (GRAF-ite): The black mineral used in pencils.

Index

barrel 4
cedar 5
eraser 11
glue 9
graphite 6, 7
lead 7

About the Author

Lori Mortensen lives in Northern California with her family and her cat, Max. When she's not tapping away at her computer, she's peeking into all sorts of fascinating subjects from butterflies to basketball—and how pencils are made!

© 2019 Rourke Educational Media

All rights reserved. No part of this book may be reproduced or utilized in any form or by any means, electronic or mechanical including photocopying, recording, or by any information storage and retrieval system without permission in writing from the publisher.

www.rourkebooks.com

PHOTO CREDITS: Cover: ©rvlsoft; p.2,4-5,14,15: ©GillTeeShots; p.2,10-11,14,15: ©DustyPixel; p.2,6-7,14,15: ©boschettophotography; p.3: ©By paulaphoto; p.8-9: ©Ryan Klos; p.12-13: ©silamime

Edited by: Keli Sipperley
Cover and interior design by: Rhea Magaro-Wallace

Library of Congress PCN Data
Peek Inside a Pencil / Lori Mortensen
(Let's Learn)
ISBN (hard cover) 978-1-64156-164-8
ISBN (soft cover) 978-1-64156-220-1
ISBN (e-Book) 978-1-64156-274-4
Library of Congress Control Number: 2017957775

Printed in Ningbo, Zhejiang, China
04-0202512936